The Miracle of Life

By Stephanie Jeffs

Illustrated by Jane Coulson

Based on Psalm 139

You created every part of me...
When my bones were being formed,
carefully put together in my mother's womb,
when I was growing there in secret,
you knew that I was there —
you saw me before I was born.

Abingdon Press

You are unique, special, different from anyone who has already been born and different from anyone who will come afterwards. There is no one quite like you. So, how did you become this very special person? How did you begin?

You began from the moment one of your father's sperm joined with an egg inside your mother. The egg and the sperm formed a tiny building block called a cell, which then attached itself to the inside of your mother's womb. This was the moment when your life began.

Over about nine months the single cell changed and developed in your mother's womb. The cell divided into two cells, then again into four. It continued to grow until there were about 100 million million cells, all joined together to become a special baby: you!

The single cell, which has been formed by the joining of the sperm and the egg, contains a special code which has the unique design for the new baby. Within one hour of the sperm and the egg joining together, all the special characteristics for a new human being have been decided.

In that hour it was decided whether you were a boy or a girl, what color hair, eyes and skin you would have, what shape your nose and ears would be, whether you would be short, medium height, or tall. These are just some of the things that make you different from anyone else.

These characteristics are inherited from your mother and father. This is the special way God planned you. You share certain characteristics with your parents and other members of your family, but each individual person is unique.

At first the new cell divides and grows until it looks like a blackberry, but it is still less than the size of the period at the end of this sentence.

Within about seven days after conception, it has attached itself to the wall of the womb so that it can begin to draw food and other good things directly from its mother. At this stage something called the placenta begins to form. The placenta's job is to act as a channel, passing food and oxygen to the baby, and taking away waste which the baby produces. The placenta also helps to protect the baby from many harmful bugs and infections.

After about five weeks you had the beginnings of a liver, brain and stomach, as well as a tail!

During the second month of your mother's pregnancy, your nose and mouth, eyes and ears were forming, and your heart began to beat.

At first you looked rather like a tadpole, but after about eight weeks, you began to look like a tiny person. Your arms and legs began to form and your tail began to disappear.

By the end of the second month of your mother's pregnancy, you were 10,000 times larger than when you were a single cell formed by the joining of your father's sperm and your mother's egg. You had the beginnings of a skeleton and your mouth had little buds where later there would be teeth.

This is the way you began. It is the way people have begun since human life began on earth.

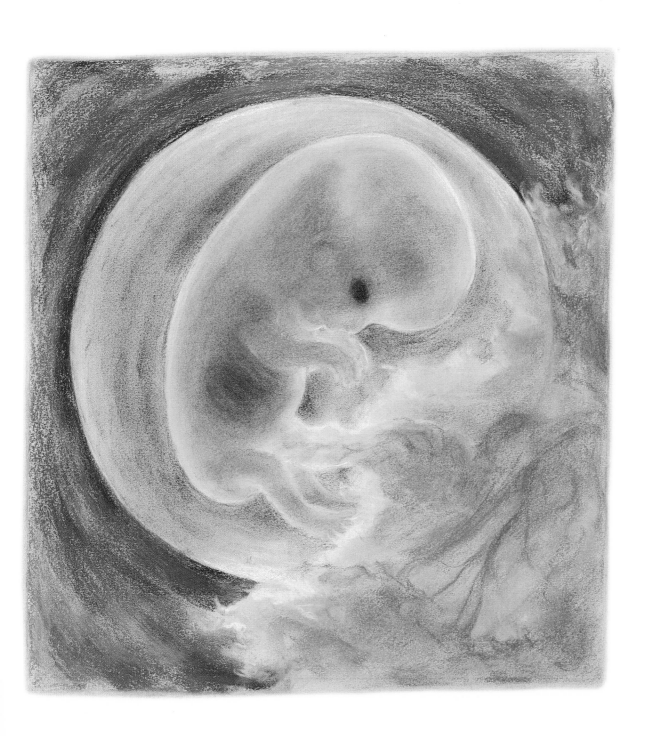

As you grew inside your mother, you were surrounded by a strong and stretchy covering, rather like a blown-up balloon. Inside this covering was some colorless liquid in which you could swim and turn somersaults. It kept you warm and safe.

Although you were developing and moving inside your mother, she probably could not feel you yet. She may not even have been certain that she was going to have a baby. But God knew all about you. God watches and cares for each tiny embryo as it moves and develops inside its mother. God already knew when and how you would move and speak, long before you were born.

Some time after the eleventh week your face began to look like a baby, with a large forehead, a small turned-up nose and a chin. Your lips were able to move, your forehead could wrinkle, and your head could turn. These were exactly the movements you were to use when you sucked milk once you were born.

As you floated in the amniotic fluid, you continued to develop.

After about four months of your mother's pregnancy, your fingernails, ears, eyes, and nose were well formed. The bones in your skeleton started to harden, and if your mother had been able to see you, she would have been able to tell whether you were a boy or a girl.

You moved about much more now and may even have sucked your thumb. You practiced the movements you would need to breathe in air once you were born, and you had taste buds on your tongue. You could now grasp the umbilical cord, the life-line which linked you to the placenta.

By the fifth month your mother began to feel you move. This was very exciting. Now she could feel you growing inside her!

At this stage you could hear and start to recognize familiar sounds and voices. There were other noises to listen to in your dark world: your mother's breathing and her heart-beat, blood rushing into the placenta and the sound of food rumblings coming from her tummy, as well as your own heart-beat. It wasn't a very quiet place!

Your muscles continued to strengthen, so that by the middle of your mother's pregnancy you could float, kick, somersault, swallow, have hiccups, get excited and calm down again! You would also have times when you were asleep and when you were awake. You even had dreams.

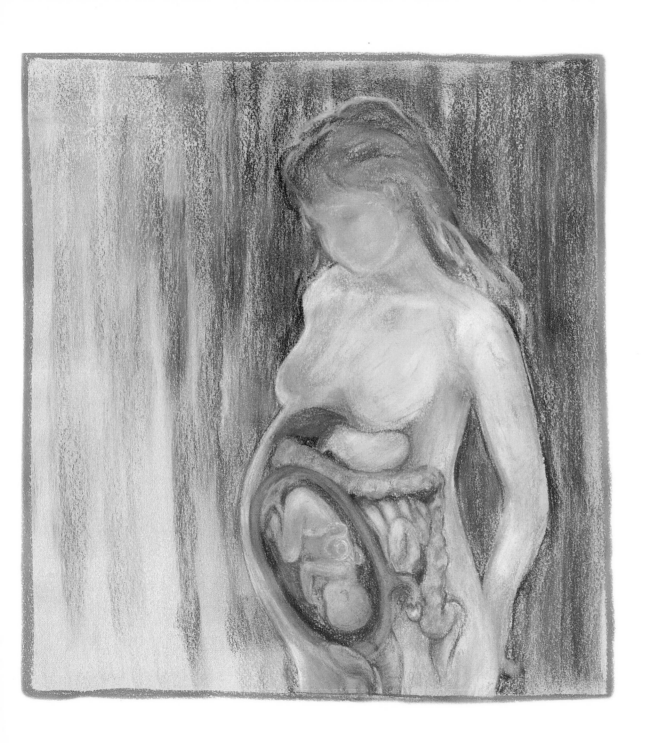

Some babies are not alone when they are developing in the womb. Sometimes, two eggs and two sperm join together at the same time. When this happens, two babies, twins, grow inside the mother. These twins will not look exactly the same. Each one will have its own placenta.

However, sometimes after an egg and a sperm have joined together to make a single cell, the cell divides into two, and two embryos develop. These identical twins share the same placenta and have many similar characteristics. Identical twins may look alike, but each one is unique. Each has its own personality and its own fingerprint.

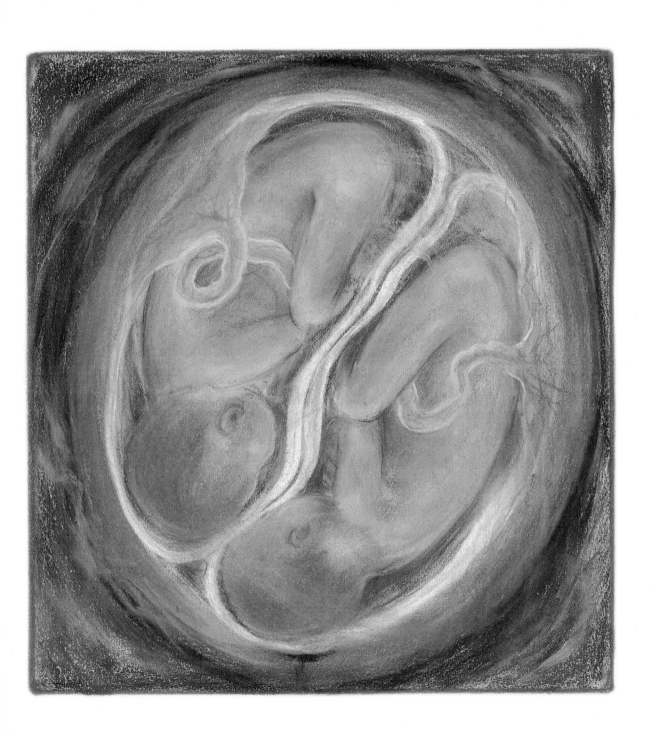

By the time you had been growing in the womb for about six months, your eyelashes and eyebrows had grown. Your body was covered in soft hair and patterns began to form on the palms of your hands. These were the beginnings of your fingerprints.

Up until now your eyelids had been shut together, but by twenty-seven weeks they began to separate so you could open your eyes.

Although it is usually best for babies to stay inside their mothers for nine months (about forty weeks), if you had been born now, with good hospital care you would have had a reasonable chance of surviving. All the important parts of your body were formed.

Your legs were bent inside the womb so that you looked as if you were sitting cross-legged upside down! You no longer had the space to somersault although you did kick and turn over. Your mother would have been able to feel your movements very clearly and you would have been able to feel her hands as she gently stroked her tummy.

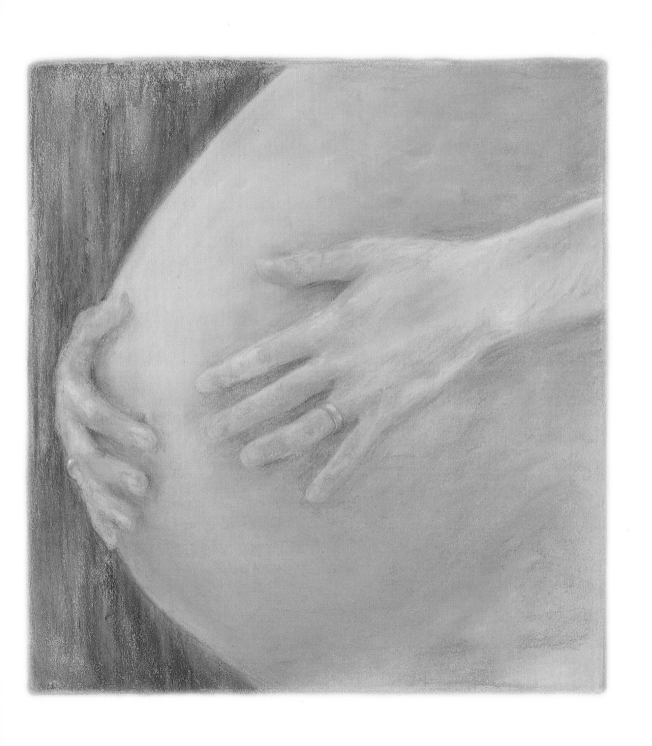

In the eighth and ninth months of your mother's pregnancy, your main job was to put on weight. You were still floating in the amniotic fluid, but there was less and less room for you to move as you grew. You were filling up the womb now, and your mother probably felt quite tired carrying you around!

While you were in the womb, you didn't need to breathe in air. Now your lungs prepared to breathe for the first time by making a frothy fluid that kept them ready for filling with air.

Your body stored a layer of fat under your skin from the food taken in from the placenta. This gave you plenty of energy after you were born.

When you were not asleep, your mother could feel you kicking. Sometimes she could feel a small hand or foot through the skin stretched across her tummy. If you had hiccups, she could feel sudden jerking movements. Sometimes you woke her up in the night by moving about inside her! Perhaps you liked the sound of music or singing and moved when you could hear it. Or perhaps you liked the lapping of warm water as your mother lay in the bath.

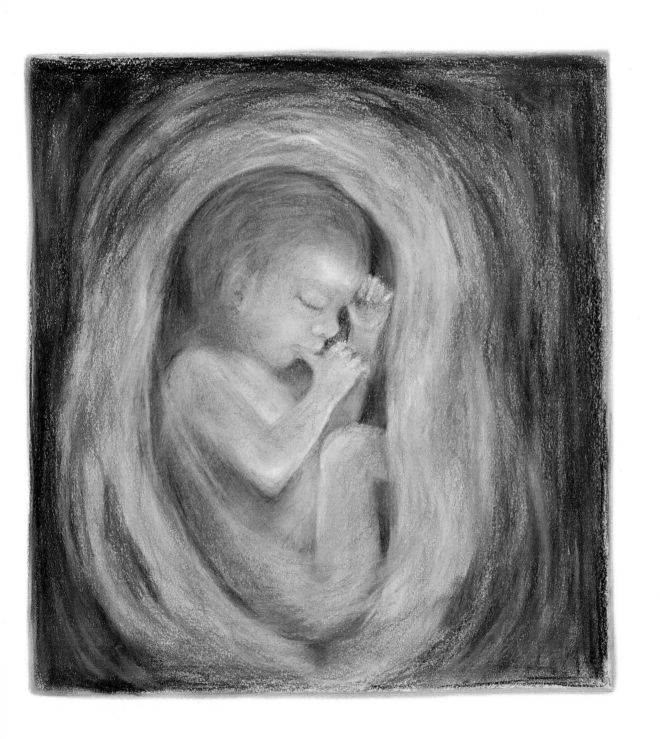

At around nine months, your body was fully developed. You knew your mother's voice and could tell when she was happy and when she was sad. You were ready to be born. Your family would be excited, looking forward to the moment when they would see you for the first time.

When your mother's body was ready, the muscles in her womb started to push you towards the opening between her legs. The muscles squeezed first tightly, then relaxed, each movement gradually taking you, head first, towards the outside world and your first breath.

Although every developing baby grows in the same way, each one is a unique creation. God makes each baby different from any other before it and any that will come after it. God knows each one before he or she is born.

As soon as you were born, you took your first breath. The umbilical cord which had been the lifeline between you and your mother was clamped and cut. After a few days, the cord shrivelled up and disappeared, leaving you with a tummy button!

Probably one of the first things your mother wanted to know was whether you were fit and healthy, and then whether you were a boy or a girl. After nine months, she could hold you in her arms and stroke your cheek. She could talk to you and sing to you as she did before, and she could call you by the special names she had chosen for you. She began to get to know you in a new and special way.

At first you needed other people to do everything for you. It would be many months before you could sit up by yourself, or crawl along the floor, or feed yourself, or walk alone. You needed lots of love and care to grow into the person you are now.

It took about 266 days for a single cell to develop into a baby.

It is a miracle.

God was with you from the moment you first began. God knew what was happening to you as you grew and developed. God was there when you were born and took your first breath. God knows you and loves you just as you are, and has made you to be a special part of creation.

This is the miracle of how you first began. It is the miracle of life.

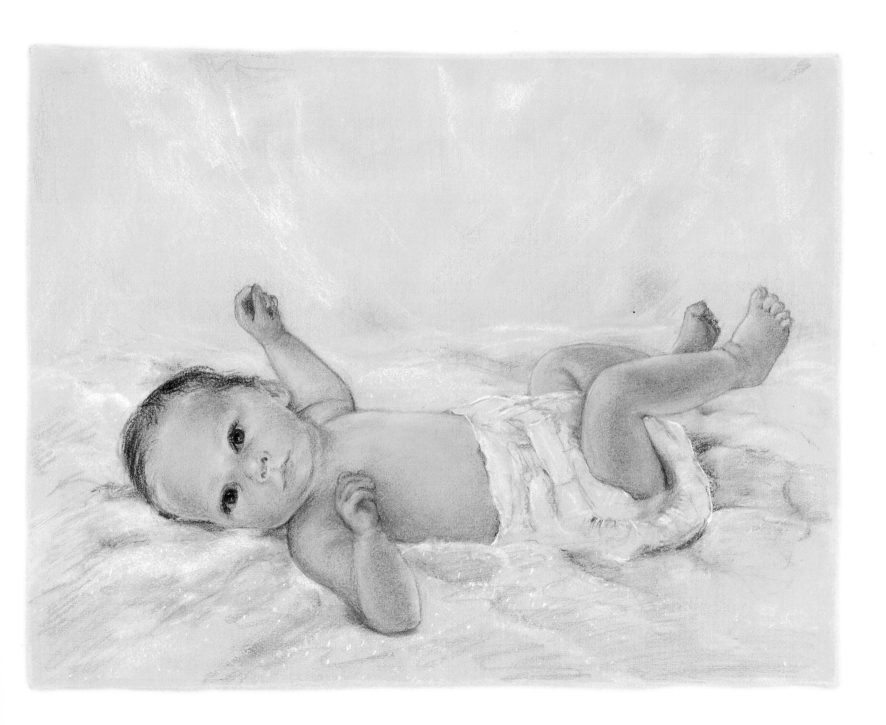

A Tamarind Book
Published in the United States of America by
Abingdon Press
P.O. Box 801
Nashville, TN 37202-0801
U.S.A
ISBN 0-687-08720-1

First edition 1998

Copyright © 1998 AD Publishing Services Ltd
Text consultants: Dr Sue Cole and Dr David Evans
Illustrations copyright © 1998 Jane Coulson
With thanks to Lennart Nilsson on whose work
some of the illustrations are based

Printed and bound in Singapore